# Onions of Glass

## By Daniel Martinez

PublishAmerica
Baltimore

Softcover 978-1-4626-4151-2
PUBLISHED BY PUBLISHAMERICA, LLLP
www.publishamerica.com
Baltimore

Printed in the United States of America

Dedication
*Wendy Dearest, oh how I love you so!*
*You, my Dearest, of women most beautiful!*
*Why, my Dearest, do you tolerate me?*
*Surely, Dearest, I contribute t'your 'nsanity!*
*And yet, Dearest, you still to me give love;*
*Yes you, Dearest, give kisses and hugs;*
*Wendy, Dearest, oh how I love you so!*
*You, my Dearest, of women most beautiful.*

*Everyone is capable of anything;*
*Anyone is capable of everything.*

*My greatest fear is that everything I know is false,*
*Knowing that that's relatively true.*

# Table of Contents

# Layers of Perception

# *To Give up a Right*

Freedom isn't free.
That's the price you have to pay.
And if it isn't,
What is, then?

Nothing, it is true;
For to make an exception
Is to pay a bill;
Or to give up a right.

What we have asked for,
We have gotten;
But what we ask for
Is gotten
At the expense
Of losing what we had.

# *Perceived Truth Perceived*

**i.**
Efficiency is a marvelous mediocrity
In which too few ever quite relish.
Excel, exceed, supersede or surpass,
The end goal is gen'rally the same.

And there's a difference between miscommunication
And a total lack thereof:
Miscomm-, then, is a result of perception
And individuals' knowledge and experience.

Success is relative to the sea-otter
Same as China-tea's overpriced cost
Bears relation to nothing at all:
Success, or lack thereof, is a perceived truth.

Perceived truth is not truth perceived
But a truth believed and, in the course,
Projected unto humanity as a whole,
Which may or may not be a good thing.

Karma does not exist,
Except as perceived truth,
Projected,
        To affect an individual individually.

**ii.**
Laziness is a malicious morbidity
In which too many too often relish.
Expel, expect, stupefied and stunned,
The end result is gen'rally the same.

And with total, lacking communication,
Perceived truth becomes truth;
At least with one there's learning.
The other, though, is debilitating.

Failure is connected to the powerful
Same as money is to the rich
And the same as war to mankind.
*Failure,* is a truth perceived:

It's all right, it's okay, you stink but anyway,
We'll excuse your laziness and stupidity
And, to make you feel much better,
We'll talk down to the intelligent.

Karma comes to exist
In bounds of this "truth" perceived,
And projected,
    To infect individuals with society.

# *Relative Perception Re: Individual*

In one instance you are the driver angry for the slow person
ahead.
In another, you are the slow person up ahead.
In another case, you are both drivers.
You don't know another person is driving that car

—you *assume.*

You cannot *see…*

But reason,

Logic,

Dictates it must be so.

Yet this person, however real,
Is in your perception
An imaginary figure.
You cannot see, but you imagine,
And that is your reality.
Even if you did not see them;
And *they* are only a perception of your consciousness,
Existing in the only way they can:
In relation to you,
As you perceive them,
Existing on your layer of perception
As your mind dictates.
Likewise the angry person behind you
When you are the slow driver.
So too the victim and perpetrator roles.
So too the righteous and the guilty.
So too the pure and the unclean,
*You* are part of the whole,
Existing for some purpose,
A vehicle for the temporary storage,

Translation,
		And release of energy.
Such is change,
		is life.

# Avadore

## *Divided*

**i.**

I didn't mean to break it,
But it just sort of happened.
(I think *it* broke *me,*
Just the same as all things.)
Can't you believe in me?
Or is that asking too much?
(I always believed in *you,*
Even when it wasn't merited.)
Are you ever so negative,
Or do you want it broken?
(I think *it* breaks *you,*
Just the same as all things.)

See you the gates of Heaven,
Or sit you before the gates of Hell?
Set a place at the wedding,
Or should I count on you being there?

Lock me in a cage
Where I let out my rage;
Give me a knife
I'll stay well alive:
Fear for all the others
Who call themselves your sisters,
Your brothers.

**ii.**

I didn't mean to break him,
But it just sort of happen'd.

                    (And I think she broke *me,*
                      Just the same as all things.)
                 Can't you read my stories,
                  Or is that asking too much?
(I always encourage *you,*
Even when it isn't merited.)
                    Are you ever so positive,
                     Or inside are you broken?
                              (I think *I* break you,
                                Just the same as all things.)


                 Look you into a great Void,
                 Or stand you before a Paradise?
                 You were there at the wedding,
                 But could you count on me being there?


                   Lock you in a cage
                 Where you let out your rage;
                   Give you back a life,
                 But not at the expense of mine:
                   Love to all the others
                 Who call themselves our sisters,
                      Our brothers.


### iii.

                 I never meant to hurt you,
                  But apparently I did;
                 And I know I didn't break you,
                 But in a way you know I did,
                   Must you do this for me,
                  And must I do that for you,
                    Or can't we just be,

Dependent upon Fate or Chance?
Always will I love you,
And hope that you will, too;
And I know you won't break me,
But in a way I know you will.


Standing there at a Fork,
How to decide left or right?
I was there at the beginning,
And I'll be there at the end;
But take a good look around:
You'll find I'm there with you still.


So grab hold of my hand
We will travel foreign lands;
Together have a life
At the expense of no one:
Love to each other,
Who call ourselves lovers.

# *The Center of My House*

A haunted house that's black and gray
Deep within there lurks decay
See the world through different eyes
Mark the skies voice alibis
Open the screen door enter
Confusion fills me I'm the center
Yet still outside yet to enter
The ceiling high and unseen
Look at the house through the screen
All of my life I've been wishing
To enter that world again.

(Lived in this house one time before
Hated it then, now I hate it more
Enter the house through the screen door
I enter my world once more)

See the cobwebs in the corner
I am the widow, the mourner
Spot the eyes within the wall
Burn me up with them I scald
Scalded by the burn I hurt
Teeth biting holes in my shirt
Open the door, steal my breath,
Overwhelming sense of dread
My breath is choked off and gone.

(Still I've yet to move beyond)

[I realize the truth pent up,
A the center I'm outside
Looking up I see the skies
Always I go everywhere,
Yet still, somehow, I stay here.]

# *The Woman in the Room*

There is a place to which I run to hide
On days with bleak gray clouds in sky,
When no one seems to be on my side,
And indeed the world's against me.
That place is not man-made
    (Necessarily);
It is the Divine-inspired grace and beauty.
It is the place where soul meets body;
Where the beast can seem a beauty;
Where all but two elements are fatuous;
And where I am the safest.

I know this place well
Though for a time I neglected it,
Allowing festering weeds to choke yard,
Allowing shutters to hang askew,
Allowing the door to creak in the wind.
The place exudes the light
    Of the thousand suns
That used to fill it—
    But that light is very dim,
    A memory of time past,
    A monument to what could have been.

One day I visited this place
And saw my beautiful abode
Was now decrepit and run down,
And I was surprised the place
    (For it looked so bad)
Was even there.

*Look at the house D built,* I thought.
But nonetheless I entered it,
To find cobwebs in corners
And paint and wallpaper peeling.
When I took a step on the stair,
It collapsed underfoot,
  And I saw the house for what it was:
  On the second floor,
  Rooms with women's laughter,
  Women's talk, womanhood.
  On the first floor,
  Rooms full of what the place had become—
    Haunted by ghosts of time past.
Then I looked up, and saw floor three,
Which was so high above me
That I despaired,
  And curled into foetal position,
  And I cried,
  And eventually I fell asleep.

At length I woke,
  But I was still in the house;
And though I tried to convince myself,
Examination of the stair showed that,
Indeed, I had not been dreaming:
The beautiful place
To which I often ran to hide,
Had fallen into terrible disrepair.

Again I despaired, crying,
But I did not ruin the floor;
And I was rewarded therefor:

For there came to me an angel,
So graceful and light, who said,
"Fear not: I will show you the way."
Nonetheless I *did* fear,
Though in her eyes was kindness,
And I could see clearly she wanted to help me.
We stood, then, staring at one another;
Then I said, "You're an angel?"
And she said, "Fear not: I will show you the way."
And I found that indeed I feared not;
And she reached out a hand to me.
I took it (it was light as a feather,
    Cool as a tombstone at night),
And a third time she said, "Fear not: I will show you the way."

Abruptly I found myself,
    The angel still with me,
In the parking lot of an apartment complex;
Quickly I realized it was our old complex;
Presently I heard a very familiar engine,
And I turned, and, lo, behold my truck,
With me driving,
    Clad in work uniform.
The angel said as I watched myself park,
"It is May twenty-fifth, two thousand-three,
The day you and A—— moved in together
Do you remember?"
    And I nodded, for I was speechless.
I watched myself get out of the car,
Watched as I went inside.
The blinds were open, the light was on,
So I could see inside:

And I saw you, so happy to se me
(Though surrounded by boxes,
And tired from all the unpacking.)
Then the angel touched my shoulder
And there was a mental montage:
A check from my father (*big*);
The guys coming over (all the time);
Me, drunk, and you caring for me;
Us, making love for the first time on that couch;
Me, with one other, on a hill, working—
Then driving away (for I'd quit);
Me, working—and then quitting, again.
And I saw myself signing books,
With you sitting in the audience so proud;
And I saw myself before the computer,
Checking the mail to see if I'd got a query
(But none ever came, of course);
Then I saw myself rejecting the queries I *did* get;
And writing (writing, writing, writing)
And I saw my one client.
And then the angel no longer touched my shoulder.
I gasped, off balance for the shock of it all,
Breathing hard, heart pounding.
Then I looked at the scene before me,
And I realized time had moved on:
No longer the twenty-fifth of May,
But the day I decided to open my publishing company:
And the angel said, "That is when it began."
I was suddenly engulfed by despair,
By sorrow—for how bad have I treated you
O how bad!

Then the angel said, "Come,"
      And although I wanted to protest,
      She had taken my hand before I could;
And we were back in the house,
At the foot of the broken stair.
Yet I saw the floor was new.
I turned to ask the angel what had happened,
But she touched my hand and we were upstairs,
Women's laughter now very clear.
I blinked, then,—
      And suddenly found myself on the first floor,
      Looking up at the angel on the second.
She looked down at me complacently,
Offering no explanation;
So I started up the stair—
      And immediately the second broke like the first.
I tried again, but the third, fourth, fifth—
      All broke likewise.
Up to the angel I looked,
      But still she offered no explanation.
      So I called to her, saying,
"What is this? How do I get to you?"
The angel nodded then,
      And I could have torn out all my hair.
"Tell me how to get up there!" I demanded;
She nodded again, still said nothing.
Furious, I could not look at her any longer;
And in my disgust, my sight happened upon the woodpile,
With the hammer and nails,
By the foot of the stair.
I looked at the angel and she nodded:
So I took up the materials,

And I rebuilt the steps,
	And then I climbed the stairs,
At the top of which awaited the angel,
Who said, "Fear not: I will show you the way."
Then she took my hand,
	And led me to the women's laughter.

No longer in the house but *our* house,
	The second one (the laughter is gone),
Both of us sitting on the couch.
I and the angel stood by the television,
Which the two of us watched so sitting:
And I heard you say,
"I have to go to Texas again."
And I heard myself argue,
But at length I conceded,
Which made the me by the tv realize my childishness,
And I recalled saying:
	"I'll have a car for you when you get back."

Then time froze:
	Everything still save the angel and myself.
She turned to me, and I to her,
And she said, "You are full of precious lies
	And empty promises, Daniel.
	You are a hypocrite,
		For you desire as she desires.
	You are blinded by illusions of grandeur,
		And refuse to see things as without a gilt edge.
	You never got the car for her.
	You worked on it, to be sure—
	But what result came of it?

You are full of precious lies, Daniel.
You are nothing but an empty promise."

The women's laughter then returned
    (For time had started once more),
And I saw us yet sitting on the couch;
Moreover that the laughter came from you,
Very faint, 'tis true, but there.
Then I began to kiss you,
And though it had been growing louder
The laughter became muffled.
I looked to the angel for explanation,
    But even as I did I realized for myself:
The laughter was inside of you,
    And I was suppressing it.

We began to make love, and I looked away.
The angel said, "Look," and I did,
    For her tone was that of command itself.
And I saw my back rippling,
Saw something moving underneath my flesh:
Then I saw your face,
    And while it had been pleased,
    Now it was contorted and angry,
    Your hazel depths now hell-fire,
    Your precious body a corpse,
    A laughing corpse and our house was as decrepit as *the*
house and there was thunder, lightning, and cackling—you,
cackling—and mice and cockroaches crawled in and out of the
walls, the sinks, the couch itself, and all over us, and yet you
laughed; your back broke—and yet you laughed; I crushed
your lungs, gave you no room to breathe, and yet you laughed;

I saw you die, I saw myself grab your spirit and hold on to it,
and yet you laughed;
     And then the rippling in my back (which I had forgotten
about) split first and then ripped open, and I shed my skin,
and I saw that I was the dragon, and my spit was to your skin
as hydrochloric acid; and my touch to you as poison, and my
juices to you as death itself.
     And I screamed, I demanded to be taken away, I turned
to the angel and pounded her chest, but she forced me to look
one last time before she would: So I looked, and, lo, behold as
I devour your flesh.
Then I turned away with a cry that tore my throat;
The angel took my hand,
And I was encompassed by blackness.
Then we were in the house,
     On the second floor.
     I was panting, trying to calm down—
     But then I realized the house was shaking!

Even without considering the angel
I ran down the stairs—
     I had to save the house!
Yet by the time I reached floor one,
The trembling had ceased.
I looked about, unsure of anything;
And when no more tremors shook the house,
I determined they would not recur.
Thus I could take in my surroundings:
     And I saw everything had fallen askew.
Upstairs went my eyes, to the angel,
To whom I said, "*Now* what?"
I did not expect answer this time,

But only a nod. Which I got,
Quickly followed by:
    "Build it up and tear it down,
    Bring it down to build it up again.
    Begin with the foundation,
        (For as you'll see, it's cracked)
        And be sure to make it level,
        And be sure to let it settle.
    The foundation thus established,
        Finish the house:
        Add the little touches that make home,
        And never take the arrangement for granted.
    The house being thus furnished,
        Build the inner walls,
        So as to define what room is where,
        And always let there be division:
            You, me, us.
    The walls being thus constructed,
        Form the outer walls,
        And be sure to include many
        *(options)*
                doors and windows:
    Thus shall you rebuild this house."

And so I did:
    I tore it down and lay foundation,
    Level, after which I let it settle;
    Then I furnished it,
    And afterward added inner walls;
    Finally the outer walls,
        Making sure of many windows and doors.
In short order I did it,

And at the end I was accosted,
And escorted to the second floor,
    By the angel.
She said, "You have done well."
And led me to the stair
(Which would take me to floor three),
At the foot of which she looked at me full on
And said, "Now you must go alone.
    The first floor is new,
    And you'll notice no women's laughter here.
    You have exorcised the ghost of time past,
    And no longer do you oppress your lover.
    Yet now you must proceed,
    Must advance to the third floor,
    Where awaits your destiny.
    Your possible future, in any case."
And then, though I'd many questions,
    Burned with curiosity,
    And fidgeted with impatience,
The angel was gone,
And I had to climb the stairs alone.

After much debate I did it
    (Though I yet struggled,
    Unsure of my strength of will,
    Afraid of the unknown,
    As I ascended);
But when I reached the top,
To find an arched door
    (Which I opened)
And a single, sun-filled room,
I pondered why I had been so nervous.

The room was absent of anything,
Save sunlight through round windows

    …(and you)

(What?
    Who?
        Where?
            When?
                How?
                    I don't understand,
                        What is this,
                            What's going on,
                                Where am I?)


So I thought:
    But yes, you were there in that sun-filled room, and your
beauty took my breath away.
You walked up to me,
    Even as I yet stood in the doorway,
And said, "Hey, Beautiful."
But could I say a thing?
    No—for my throat had closed,
    And I was speechless.
You said, "Look at the house D built.
    So fine its construction,
    So well-crafted the little thing!
    So open though it is closed,
    So precious to me,
        Because you made it.
And here am I,
    The woman you've been waiting for."

Finally I found my voice, and I said,
    "And I am here for you."
Then you enfolded me in your arms,
And in them I found all I had lost;
And I realized my place, my house,
Is not so much a place:
It is a symbol, which houses my true home.
For there is a place to which I run to hide
On days with bleak gray clouds in sky,
When no one seems to be on my side,
And indeed the world's against me.
That place is not man-made
    (Necessarily),
But Divine inspired grace and beauty.
It is the place where soul meets body;
Where the beast can seem a beauty;
Where all but two elements are fatuous;
And where I am safest.

*Avadore*

**i.**
The woman.
The woman in the room of that house,
That house gotten to by way of I-10 West,
Then follow the Dead Road to the abandoned place,
Edge of civilization, brink of cotton fields.

In the room she sits,
A broken creature in a dilapidated structure
With cracked walls and spiders' webs,
Broken window panes, rat droppings,
The light carcasses of hundreds of roaches.

Her eyes are gouged out,
She is in the northeast corner so limp;
Dried gore caked upon cheeks so pale,
Hair once luxurious now falling out,
Limbs once strong lie broken, useless at her side.

Dressed in a dress, as little girls.
So aged the thing, so old.
In the heat she does not decay;
Only dries to an ash-y crisp.
    And alone she sits,
        With a story to tell,
            But no one to whom to tell it.

**ii.**
The couple.
The couple at the funeral,

That of her uncle so distant but—
Yes, odd, but he'd left her something;
So come they had, dressed to nines,
Showing up early but last nonetheless.

Long and slow the procession,
Long-winded priest, fake tears accompanying loud sobs.
*No one really cares,* he thought:
*They're like us, come to see what they can get.*

For whom, then, is the show of sorrow?
For the priest? Who could care less, so to speak?
For the family? All know one another,
All know one another's virtues and vices;
So why hide them? To pretend normalcy?
For their god? But it would know better.

So thought he, Daniel Adam, while couched
Uncomfortably betwixt Aunt Jane and lovely Ava.
Ava's dead uncle, Ava's fat aunt, Ava his wife.

And afterward they shuffle out, so feeble,
So distraught at such a loss:
And thoughts immediately turn to executor.
When the will-reading? —In a few days.
So what to do 'til then? —Visit the family.
Yay, great, drunken fun with a bunch of hypocrites!
Last checked, everyone's idea of a good time.

Depressing, the funeral, true—
But for the loss, or the familial presence?
Oh such thoughts kept Adam to himself!

For a few days later he was no better—
There at the reading of the will,
Anticipating eagerly what was to be had.
And they got the house!
What house? Old, abandoned, decrepit—
What a house!

**iii.**
The house.
The house so old, decrepit, decayed.
Invited to visit, the whole family;
For which Ava was hopeful, Adam doubtful.
Not now, of course, but later, after the rebuilding.
Of course.

What's the point, though? To live there?
Not to live there—to rent it out, silly.
Such is said between the couple:
And although he's misgiving, he agrees.
Of course.

Ah, the house, gotten to so simply:
I-10 West, a stretch of highway
With lots of mesquite and small businesses;
A bit of corporation, a good authority:
Exit Dead Road, make a left at the sign;
See the hot dog vendor—Gone;
Cotton fields? Skydiving? Airport?
See all those normal things?—Gone,
Passed by, not in a flash but without a thought
—That they mightn't see such things again.

Of course.

So the threshold is passed;
The corner store is come upon:
And strange the clerk, but affable,
Having some salt with his pepper
And blanks within shingles of rotting teeth:
A gentle demeanor to offset the "off".

Down the road with some soda and candy and chips,
Pass the old cotton mill—by itself,
Standing so alone and rusted metal:
But in the back a hundred cars,
New and old and high and low-end;
Who knew where they came from?
                              Oh, Ava.

Hang a right after half a mile,
Follow the broken road to its end:
Starting with a brick-post mailbox 40-20,
A tree fence—cottonwood trees, of all things;
A flat-dirt drive with patches of dying grass left and right.

The house ahead, surrounded by dead oleander;
A tree to its right, a tree to its left:
Dead, while all others lived:
For lining the west border, a tree-fence;
To the back, north, nothing but sky;
Eastward a wire fence with state signs;
And then,
Of course.

Broken windows and hanging shutters,
No door that latched or locked,
No running water, but dripping from faucets,
Maddeningly so
…Of course.

Well, it's a fixer-upper. Not too much to it, really.
                                        Oh, Ava.


**iv.**
Ava.
Oh, Ava: What find you here?
Oh—remember when you left Adam?
Why'd you leave?
                        —Because he'd been with another.
Why'd you return?
                        —Because he'd changed.
Then what is he doing, Ava? Look, look!

Oh, and she looks, and what is he doing?
    He's ripping out her heart and walking on it
    As it lies on a bed of coals and broken glass:
So she feels, for there he is with the other,
That bitch that slut that whore:
How did she get there with them?
    (She's not there.
        Oh, Ava. She's not there.)


But—oh!—remember when Billy died?
                *(No!)*


Yes—when he was coming to pick you up

You were drunk as a skunk and he was saving you;
And then he got hit by a drunk driver
      (I didn't know he was coming!)
—He didn't survive the wreck, did he?
      (I thought he was mad at me!)
You thought he wouldn't come, Ava,
Because you don't know family; you know no love.
      (I never meant to!
      It was an accident!)
Fine, an accident: Through which came Adam,
The lawn-boy at the graveyard, yes?
So: What if you lost Adam?
      (I would find him!)
How would you find him?
      (I'd kill my brother!)

                              Oh, Ava.
                  Ava.
            Oh, Ava.

How broken you lie when Adam finds you.
How overjoyed by his presence;
But look: That's an axe in his forehead!
And that's his blood all over you!
Ava, what have you—

Hello, Ava.
      So says Adam, who is fine.
And she's confused: Dead, or alive?
Real, or unreal? Friend or enemy?

Ah—the blank slate, the bare *tabula rasa.*

Time frozen, and Adam with it:
And the whole environment with him;
And the color fades, as on a television,
And it's all black and white but no—
Ava, no, oh no, Ava: It's not black and white:
                                    It's ash!


Touch, yes: Your tears stop nothing.
Their moisture cannot solidify such light substance.
And everything crumbles around you.
So what is left?
        —The woman.
            Who is she?


**v.**
Adam found.
Adam found the woman first,
Found her by accident looking for Ava.


Oh, why had they to fight?
So she wanted to fix up the house,
Fix it and rent it out. It was a good idea.
    So why reject it? Because it was hers.
            Not trying to, but feeling jealous.
Always he'd been so—one of his flaws.


So he'd stormed out, left her there,
All alone in the decrepit old house,
And got all the way to the corner store.
There he stopped, for gas:
And headed right back to the house.

But Ava was gone, or hiding.
Where was she?
     (In her own hell.)

So he looked for her, and found:
The room, top o' the stair, all the way right,
At hall's end the entrance to *her* room.

So he found her, eyes gouged,
Limbs limp and broken, useless:
Who did this to her, now? Or what?
Then the door to the room slammed shut,
And they were alone,
And she was alive or at least she moved;
And she asked where she was,
And who he was, and if he was cold;

So childish, her voice.
Yet a woman she was:
And this Adam saw then, for she was alive!

The corpse rising, blood crusted, arms useless,
Crick-crack-crinkle as bones mended,
Roll the head on the neck to loosen kinks,
Like a breathing, living machine she jerked;
And such a bloody mess her shirt!
     For the blood was fresh, again,
     Running down cheeks like rivers,

And he stepped toward her—
                              *squish!*

One of her eyes underfoot.

So he looked around, saw a new room,
A working room—so bloody!
The walls cracked and bleeding like her sockets,
The carpet matched, for it was soaked through;
And the sheets messy, with blood and
Oh—the pungent odor!
       Of sex, of fear;
 Of regurgitation, as Adam did so.


And urine, and shit, and semen and blood:
And then Adam saw visions:
Her father, Ava's uncle, having his way with her
While she lay, bound hands and feet, unable to stop him.


Gagged she could not scream;
 So large her father she could hardly breathe.
  So scared she that she was beautiful;
And, Adam saw, she was beautiful anyway.


Then her father shuddered on top of her,
And rolled off of her, and left;
 She lay there, crying, bleeding,
Unable to close legs for the ropes.


Adam looked on, not pervertedly but paralyzed.
How could anyone do such a thing? And,


Remotely,
Was the family's sham at the funeral for this?
For neither priest nor God, but for shame?
 She was beautiful, and probably intelligent,

Had hopes and desires and fears and much to learn—
And that man was taking it from her!

Her own father was destroying his creation—
And for why? Because she reminded him of someone?
Because he hated himself? Bec—

Hey, who's there!
                    (And her father returns)

Who's where? Adam wonders. Is this some sort of game?
But no, Father eyeballs Adam and lumbers toward,
Angry, scary, aggressive: And Adam stands.
Not in defiance, but still paralyzed, shocked.

A demand of information, but somehow—
Somehow when Adam answers, blood gurckles out,
In place of words thought to be said:
    Causing Father to say, "Ha! You are with *us,* now!"
Then look at Adam as if he'd said nothing at all:
And Adam realized the man *had* said nothing:
The house had just spoken through him.

And where was Ava? Adam knew not;
But the father looked toward the bed,
The woman looked to Adam for salvation,
His paralysis was broken and he charged,
Beating the man's head with fists,
Hitting ears and neck and, once,
Accidentally a kick to the naked scrotum.
Down for the count so Adam looked to the woman
—Who was, surprise, surprise, free of her binds:

Such that Adam realized it was a show.

For she was beautiful again, and happy,
As though nothing had happened:
But a look showed the father, still passed out;
Now she was calling him, Adam, Adam,
Come to me, Come into me, Come in me.

And he felt a stirring, he felt no control,
Lost in his own body, fooled by his own senses;
And knew it was her, that he was helpless to resist;
So he was lured, to her, to her kiss, to her sex.

And he thought he saw Ava watching,
Wanted to say it wasn't happening, not now or again,
But then she was gone and Adam, as he came in her,
Realized he'd never see her again:

Then the woman gouged out his eyes,
Bony thumbs into soft flesh;
And there was a churning round his manhood:
And he realized she was *eating* him,
Consuming him, combining him with her self.

And his last thought, as walls cracked;
As she cackled, as blood ran down his cheeks, was:

Oh, Ava.

Ava.

Oh, Ava.

**vi.**
Ava and the woman.
Ava and the woman stood facing each other,
Ava alive, the woman looking quite like a living corpse.
All had crumbled around Ava:
All the ash blew away in the wind.

Wind that existed but that Ava felt not:
For she was inside, at the center,
In the middle of this, her paradigm.
Who was she? So asked Ava,
And the woman answered, "I am you."
No you're not!

"Oh, but I am: You made me, at the funeral.
…Remember? The brother you killed,
Driving so drunk as you had?
And at the funeral you met Adam,
…Remember?
   (Of course.)

Adam, the first man to love you for you:
For your father loved your body, but not you.
And your mother never protected you.
You lost your brother, you met Adam
Then—you lost Adam.

…Remember? You wanted to buy a house,
Fix it up and then rent it out. You fought about it,
Adam left you, but came back—
But you were gone, by then:
   And you trapped him, you killed him:

And he knew, knew what you were doing,
But he didn't fight, because you created *him,* as well.
      *(No!)*


**vii.**
Oh, Ava.
The woman in the room of that house,
Edge of civilization, brink of cotton fields.
She'd tried to break the walls but they bled.
She tried to break windows but water flooded.
      Tried to set fire all around, but nothing stayed lit.
      So she ran herself into a wall at full speed,
      Breaking one limb at a time, one bone at a time.
      *After* she'd taken her eyes out, of course.
            Of course.


Now, she sits.
: …Dried and old and dead.
Hidden from the world in that house,
: …The one that no one visits.
So aged, the thing. So old.
      In the heat she does not decay;
            But only dried to an ash-y crisp.
And alone she sits,
With a story now told,
But no one to listen to it.

## *The Girl Who Wasn't There*

She said I don't know about us moving in;
So he went to find himself a new friend,
Getting down hard on himself
For wrongs perceived as his perpetration and
> *(Perceived truth is not truth perceived.)*

In the end, wishing he'd just make right:
For in spite of recent argumentation,
His job he well-liked, loved he his woman,
And losing neither was his intention
> (Nobody needs you, damned fool).

But he was in an oddly calm mood,
Thinking many desperate thoughts
Whilst driving aimless through town,
> *(In one instance, you are the driver)*

When he decided to buy the groceries:
So to the supermarket he went,
Beginning to notice his own odd mode
But quite incapable of altering it:
His body a ship, his mind its passenger
> (The world turns without you).

Then, there in the produce section,
A uniquely attractive, new friend.
Had she been there a moment ago?
So wondered he, but did not fret too much.
  Pass by the oranges and lemons and lettuce,
  Tomatoes and onions, mushrooms, herbs,
  Looking at his list as he passed each one by,

When, alas, he heard from not too far off,
                    (Though it would be nice to be needed)

"Um, excuse me?" and he looked up.
There was the girl-woman he'd seen,
And—"Are you talking to me?" he asked
—And she was looking at him?!
        With big blue lovely eyes, a tongue stud;
        Such pale skin and dark black-brown hair,
        Perfect contrastifications, for her,
        Dressed in blue and so gorgeous
                    (Even it was a superficial need).

Then she asked what veggies he ate,
Because she'd been charged with the dinner
And there, back at the house
                    (sigh),
Was a bunch of guys hanging out.
        No, she'd never cooked much before;
        What was she making? —Jambalaya,
        From a box, so sensually said she.
        He said, "Guys don't eat veggies."
                    (But does that sound crazy?)

Thereafter he made some suggestions,
Then went he to get some lemons;
For another approached her,
Offering to assist as needed;
        But she wanted it not, he could see:
        She had needed him, specifically.
        Smugly thought, he returned to his cart
        —And saw there was no one to be found
                    (Yes).

# Glass Onion

# *Prologue*

Let's go back, then, in our minds
To the first man in his prime.
No, I don't mean Adam *per se,*
So let's call him
    (Mada, Madra, Magra, Magda,)

                          …Madeira
                    Mage*i*ra, the Man.

Wait.               …No.
          Let's go unto even the beginning,
The time time began.
    …The time *it* all began.


Which came first, the chicken or the egg?
O, the beautiful implications thereof!
Where, indeed, did the *stuff* originate
To become all the *stuff* of today?
The answer, of course, is the God(s).
Whether the God(s) be an exact, measurable, knowable,
    perceivable entity of modern science
    —Or the mystical Being(s) so said to be,
For our purposes and for argument's sake,
From the God(s) do all things emanate.

# *Existence*

In a room all alone,
    Four walls a floor and a ceiling,
    Lieth on the floor Conscious Being.
    Awake, seeing, perceiving?
    Aware of what is before it—
        But can it see?
    —If not sight, then sound.
    Or taste, or feel.
…Does consciousness breathe?
Sensation determines consciousness.
If there is no sensation, what is there?
No hear, see, touch, taste?

                      What, then?
Time, light, matter, space;
Energy is *matter* times the speed of *light,* squared;
And there is no speed without time,
    Neither lacking space.
Existence is pure energy, trapped.
    Confined. Held? Willfully present?
Perception is awareness of such existence;
For, it's not that nothing comes from nothing,
But that there is nothing without a consciousness to perceive
it;
Which can only perceive if aware of itself;
Which it can be only insofar as sensation stimulates,
Which can only stimulate if the sensation can be perceived,
Which can be perceived only if it exists as a thing-in-itself
    outside the consciousness but within the conscious,
    perceptive realm.

Nietzsche says there is the master and the slave,
Where master measures good and bad in the sense that:
"Good = success, popularity, wealth, power, *et cetera*"; and
"Bad = the opposite.", as opposed to the slave, who measures
*Good* as charity, humility, kindness, *et cetera*, and
*Bad* as aggression, excess, the general opposite of good,
Even as the slave-mentality creates merely a lesser slavery.
      In the absence of *material* goods and power,
            Emphasis is placed upon individuality and humanity;
                  Take for example the feudal society.


Now, freedom is access to both material and abstract,
Not forced to deal with one or another specifically or
particularly.
This leads to a contradiction within self, where:
I am master, I am slave,
      I am subject to myself, I am subject to no one or -thing.
            Realization: *The same is true of you.*
      Relative conclusion: You can only reject society when it is
so advanced as to allow individual independence therefrom;
The socio-anarchic commune is only temporarily possible,
      Only partially attainable by a temporary group.
We can cultivate and hunt to feed ourselves,
Also clothe and defend, shelter and so on;
Yet hard labor is not conducive to intellectualism,
Such that the commune and its *option* should exist,
As a sort of temporary "adult summer camp".
Ideally, all who attend, even if temporarily,
Would adhere to some transcendentalist philosophy.
Understand: intellect may or may not be stimulated,
But in the course of things, absolute freedom can be achieved.
To choose an environment in which the intellect may thrive,

Is to compromise one's freedom.
Are your blood cells or brain considered slaves to the body?
—Yes and no;
Being so related as they are, both sides can be effectively argued.
So too humans' "enslavement" to
Nature, Earth, God, Self, whatever.
Consciousness, freedom, intellect, individuality—
All leading to a breakdown of the *whole*.


There is no morality,
Except as a construct of the individual society of the individual.
The same is true of the superman or overman:
For value is determined thereby, as well.
And also God—religion in general.
Now, even if we exist with very little intellectual stimuli,
Farming the land, hunting, and so on—
Living as primitively as is comfortably possible—
There is still *group* and *self-preservation*.
…Self preservation is a direct result of:
One's perceived obligation(s) to self and group:
Death is change, change is death.
…Yet, self-preservation is a direct result of consciousness,
Where, *because* of the consciousness,
Certain freedoms have been forfeited and one is, therefore,
Always defending what is left.
*(Freedom isn't free.)*
It is the mentality not of the perpetrator, but the victim;
Not the free man, but the enslaved,
Who is awed by the vastness of
*(freedom)*

existence.

So awed by the enormous,
And minuscule, effects s/he can have on it,
Being a part of it even as it stands alone, on its own.
And so eager to participate,
        That he holds himself in check,
        Protecting the existence *from* him but also *him* from *it.*
        Oh lawlessness and the possibilities you represent!
Yet, this would presuppose the existence of various abstracts,
And furthermore the existence, in humans,
        Of morality and various, basic truths and concepts,
        Prior even to physical conception;
Perception, then, would be composed of so many *abstracts,*
Such as power, wealth, happiness,
        Pleasure, plain, loss, gain, and so on.
…One's sense of self is rooted in the individual
Master-moralistic mentality, relative-slash-subject to
The universe, which is the greater
forcerealityunitexistenceentity.
…Consciousness is that by which we have:
        Access to both the material and the abstract.
        Consciousness, then, is freedom; and
        Perception is realization of consciousness.

# *Nothing*

The dialectic is based on three concepts:
That everything [perceived] is comprised of opposites;
That gradually one overcomes the other;
That change moves in spirals, not circles.
Relative proof of this may be shown thus:

$$1 + 1 = 2$$
$$2 + 1 = 3 \; ; 2 - 1 = 1 \; ; 2 \text{ x } 1 = 2 \; ; 2 / 1 = 2 \; ;$$
$$1 / 2 = .5 \; ; .5 + 2 = 2.5 \; ; 2 - .5 = 1.5 \; ; 2 \text{ x } .5 = 1 \; ;$$
$$2 / .5 = 4 \; ; 1 - 2 = -1 \; ; .5 - 2 = -2.5 \; ; -1 \text{ x } 2 = -2 \; ; -1.5 \text{ x } 2 = -3$$
$$3 + 1 = 4 \; ; 3 + 2 = 5 \; ; 3 \text{ x } 2 = 6 \; ; 3 - 1 = 2 \; ; 3 \text{ x } 1 = 3 \; ; 3 / 1 =$$
$$3 \; ;$$
$$1 / 3 = .33 \; ; .33 + 3 = 3.33 \; ; 3.33 \text{ x } 2 = 6.66 \; ; 3.33 + 4 = 7.33$$
$$;$$
$$4 + 5 = 9 \; ; 9 - 2 = 7 \; ; 7 \text{ x } .5 = 3.5 \; ; 9 + 2 = 11 \; ; 9 + 7 = 16 \; ;$$
$$9 - 7 + 2 \; ; 7 + 7 = 14$$

*Nothing* is an absolute lack of any physical substance or consciousness;
An idea, rather than manifest,
     created to understand vast spaces, and small spaces,
Such as distance, size, stillness, relativity and-or relation,
        and so on.
The *concept of zero* is just that:
        a concept.
Grammatically, *nothing* is properly an adjective,
Being a noun only insofar as an idea is a *thing*.
It is not possible to see *negative one*.
It is possible to see *one less,* but in life,
The perceived death is zero,

And continued existence thereafter negative one and counting.
From this it would follow that positive numbers
Are somewhat equivalent to life and conscious, perceptive, reality,
And negative numbers to life after death, other than one's own,
But not because of any relation to the "goodness"
Of a "positive" or "negative" number.
As far as conscious beings are concerned,
Nothing can be *only* an idea,
Therefore all conscious reality is relative, is a positive number;
But all that exists of its own accord is a negative integer,
Which includes but is not limited to:
Wealth, the material assessment of well-being
Relative in conscious reality to perceptions thereof;
Power, the ability to control or force
Relative to perceptions thereof;
And deadly sins and defensive virtues,
And all heroic and cowardly traits.

$(-1) \times X = -X$
Zero is greater than negative one is greater than negative two; but
$-1 \times -1 = 1$

I am not one.
*I* am zero.
*You* are one, another in addition to me.
But *I* am a concept, as is zero…
You are one, therefore the product of two negative principles,

Likely matter and consciousness.
Perception of you allows, or causes,
For acknowledgment of my Self and Existence,
    As *another*.

           *Then* I am one,
Where you are matter (-1)
    Multiplied by my consciousness (-1);
Zero now represents the difference(s) between us,
Whether it be sight, smell, taste, touch or sound,
Space, distance, time, or whatever else.


$I = 0$; (yo)$U = 0$;
    $0 =$ Nothing, nonexistence, non-consciousness.
    $0 = -1$, since outside the conscious realm all is a negative
integer.
    I, -1, times U, -1, = One Reality.
Within this single reality,
    $I = 1$ and $U = 1$;
    Together, in one reality, two perceptions.
    These two perceptions, within the single reality,
    Are two sub-realities ($2 \times 1, 2 / 1$).
Linguistic communication is equivalent to mathematical
division:
When I communicate with you, or you with me,
The two sub-realities are predominated by one or the other (2
/ 1)
And, having shared part of myself with you,
    *Half* is the result ($1 / 2 = .5$); that is,
        You now know yourself,
        But also you have a perception of me,
        Which can essentially be only half-true,
            Since you are not me.

Each of us now has approximately one and a half realities,
                                    Odd as that sounds.
It is separate, because the communication is change,
Organizedfiledtracked by the consciousness present
*As* a change so that, previously,
This *was* the case, but presently *this* is the case.
Now there are two negative integers within one conscious
reality,
Existing separately relative in two sub-realities,
Each with a *memory* of their individual sub-realities but
present,
With essentially half-perceptions due to the chaos of change
                        Invoked        by        their
communication,
In again one, single reality (.5 + .5 = 1);
Along with a new, "quarter", perception:
                            That of the future.
Based on past experience,
    It may be supposed the same will happen again (.5 x .5 =
.25);
And whether or not the thing happens lends itself to intuition
        One reality,
                Half of which is perception (of past and
present),
One-quarter of which perception is supposition (of future—
reason),
One-sixteenth of which is intuition (instinct, base knowledge,
etc.);
—So that one-eighth of supposition is intuition;
Is one-sixteenth of perception,
    Where *supposition* is one-quarter of it,
    And perception is only half the true reality.

                    Reality is unknowable without a consciousness,
Or without at least two conscious beings,
So that each half-reality equals one reality.
Change *is* spiraling, because *my* one reality,
    Half the true reality,
Is composed of these things,
                                        as is yours,
So that, essentially, together we *perceive* one-quarter of "true"
reality.
That being the case, together we *know* but one-sixteenth of it,
Understand insofar as we can suppose this or that future
    Only one-thirty-second of it,
        And intuit but one sixty-fourth of true reality.
And the amount we are able to know, or suppose,
 Diminishes in groups of more than two conscious entities,
As well as upon merely further consideration:
For if together we know one-sixteenth of reality,
Then truly we know one thirty-second,
    One sixty-fourth,
        One hundred-twenty-eighth,
            And so on.
We can never *know* anything of "true" reality,
    Truth, power, will, et cetera, *while existing consciously.*


…Everything is relative to perceptions, or ideas,
Of *excess* and *sufficiency.*
For example, the need, want, or desire, for or of, power or
wealth,
    Sloth or diligence, and so on,
        Are relative to excess and sufficience.
Being *zero,* any existence is excessive;
Being -1, any existence is zero, as in: a *concept;*

And -1 is sufficient in itself;
And being 1, existence is manifestation of self.
Consciousness, is the filter.
It is the means of organizing.
To be conscious is to *order;*
Consciousness *is* time, as in order,
Since nothing can be ordered lacking chronology.
    Even that which seems utter chaos,
    Had a beginning.
Energy is mass times the speed of light squared;
    There is not speed without space and time;
    There is nothing without a consciousness.


…But we can reproduce.
Re-create the beginning.
Reproduction is the creation of consciousness.
    —But not really.
We've the *means to allow* for the
                  *coming into existence* of consciousness,
But do we really *create* our offspring's consciousness?
    Did my parents *give* me my consciousness,
        Or did I always have it, by merit of existing?
The *choice* of our consciousness is selfish:
    We simply are. I simply am.


    …Well, then: Why must the abstract be ordered?
Fine if I simply exist,
But why am I an agent of order?
*Am* I an agent? Is that my purpose?
Or am I the God(s)?
    —Who knows if there is a *reason* for consciousness?

Presumably, "knowing" all these things,
    I am "enlightened":
    I could consider myself one with the universe;
        But why did I manifest myself in the first place?
All I know is my existence here.
My parents have memories of when I was young,
But that's relative and I have my own.
Each manifestation, or every thing I perceive as existing,
Is an attempt to understand myself.
In my life, all that which interests me,
Or makes me happy, is purposeful:
For that is that for which I was "meant".
And so the same of you.
In friends and family,
One finds common factor,
Which affirms concept of self—
Beginning, past, and present—
Communication the means of so knowing.

…If truth was known by all,
Then n'one would exist.
That is why truth is so debatable.

…All that I perceive is composed of two parts
Only insofar as one part is the external (positive) object,
And the other is the abstract (negative) with which it is
associated.

If the world outside my consciousness
Is "opposite" the true reality,
    Then therein
The law would not be: Opposites attract,

But: Like attracts like,
Or: Self is attracted to self.
The idea or perception that opposites attract
Can be related to the duality of perception,
Being presented solidly
	Even as it is abstract-plus-concrete.


…What do we, as conscious beings,
	Seek, or seek to do?
Truth. Why?
	—Because reality is a lie.
Sensation. Why?
	—Because reality is senseless.
Order; because reality is chaos.
Knowledge; because reality is void.
The sun; because reality is cold.
	And so on and so forth.
In reality, then, there is nothing.
	Reality is zero.
	*It* is a concept,
		As am I;
				And my perceived world,
	All real and existing independent but relative,


Is all that I know.
—But why am I manifest in the first place?
	—To learn, perhaps, but why else?
Honestly, the answer may be accessible only by the perceived
death.
Really, it doesn't matter, anyway:
As far as I know, I have lived,
	And will continue to live, forever.

I am taught that I was born,
But that only explains me to myself;
And the rest of things follows similarly.
It is said we live our lives in a day an hour a minute;
    Can we deny it?
There are skeptics because I doubt myself;
Drunks because I drank alcohol;
Leaders because I am aware of my self in relation to existence;
A cellulous mass of humanity, because I have a body;
    But that humanity is often confused,
    Panicked, excessive, or just plain wrong:
    Relative to the brain's,
        Or consciousness's,
    Perception that reality is a lie.
I am prone to group because in life or consciousness,
    *I,* as all things, am divided;
And to individuality because I am all that exists.
I will tend to dominate because I *am* all that exists,
    Yet my perception of you contradicts this and I,
    Unable to deny what I perceive,
    Seek nonetheless to normalize insofar as I possibly can.
I communicate because I am conscious;
    Because in reality there is no need of communication.
The abstracts that exist in reality
Manifest in the form of the various groups,
To which I may or may not adhere,
From which I gain knowledge of myself,
With which I define myself.
In reality there is I,
    And all the things I am.
I can walk up to,
    And *into,*

the sun.
That, however, is a perception.
Memory-Time-Space-Consumption-
Transformation of Energy.
Time then exists,
Because I, conscious,
Recorded walking up to the sun.
Time, space, matter and light perceived, energy,
consciousness.
I *am* the Big Bang,
And "0" is a flat, two-dimensional
Misrepresentation of the *spiral* of life,
Of change, of consciousness, of existence.

# *Individuality*

Let us recall Mageira, our symbolic first man.
Mageira the Man has no color;
Which is not to call him an albino,
But to imply a lack of race.
For our purposes, this Mageira
Possesses already a vast knowledge;
Of the sun and its celestial cohorts;
Of all that the earth brings forth;
Of that which binds and propels men to and from a task;
Of what practices gain him popularity;
Of what practices gain him favor;
  Which we call Astrology or Religion,
  And Agriculture and Farming,
  Politics, Economy, and Education
           (generally).


Yet for even Mageira there came an end;
At which his family he called to bed,
Saying, "Come, that I may tell you;
Allow me, you who so love me,
To teach you, whom I myself so love.
Lean close, for I'll speak low.
Listen close;
   I'll never be able to tell you again."
And the family gathered 'round;
And they leant close, to hear him;
And closely they listened, hanging on ev'ry word,
Knowing they would never hear it again.

He said:

Everything exists of its accord,
In its own realm, where it is individual,
And all things else are perceived as relative,
Not it to them, but the opposite.
It is important to know:
Each thing is distinctive on its own;
And relative to the perceiver.
      Yet, there are concrete things to see,
      As well as invisible, abstract things.
The concretes are all things seeable
      Not by only one, but at least two, people;
Whereas Abstracts are all things imaginable,
      And that is simply that.


Now, the individual realm, as such,
Is created and continuously altered,
Both consciously so, and sub-,
Through the individual *perception*
Which is initially blank, presumably—
Which is not to assume that babies have no knowledge,
      But simply lack knowledge of the knowledge they possess,
Being ruled almost entirely by Abstracts
            And the various bodily functions.
That is the world…
                        That is…the world,
If you think about it:
                        Full of objects,
Which exist according to function,
Without knowing of their own existence.
…The *First Knowledge* must be
Pain and pleasure variously perceived,
Which forevermore is the basis of

The individual's concept of "good" and "bad",
Whether such associations are related
Either directly or indirectly,

                                     Consciously or sub-.

The First Knowledge, then,
Stems from the art of association
    (Where *genius* is beautiful art
    And *idiocy* a most distasteful piece),
The first conscious associations of good and bad
    Being of pain or pleasure, in addition to awareness via the
senses.
It must be rather tempered, however,
By one's bodily functions,

                                 In that

Hunger and food may be associated,
And bowel movement and subsequent relief,
But not the two processes' relation to each other;
Or, if these *are* the first conscious realizations,
    Then is all subsequent view of the world tempered
        By the need to eat, shit, and piss?
Either way, we cry in communication,
Leaving it to the caretakers to fix us;
And complaint, most assuredly,
Is associated with early perceptions

                              Of communication,

As well as how perceived problems are solved.
…Also irreversibly linked is laughter,
To perhaps somewhat of a lesser extent;
The First Knowledge seeming, therefore,
To be comprised of the art of association
As well as of communication.

                             …This being the case,

It is worthy to note the variety, good or bad,
Of environments in which to be reared—
As unique as the individual! Indeed,
That *is*, largely, *the* uniquity thereof!
…In any case, it's that First Knowledge,
Our first impressions and sensations,
Which gradually, and with time, transform,
That allow for such a thing as perception;
 For obviously I don't mean what is seen,
 But rather the context in which it is seen:
 That which causes disgust in one mind,
 But fascination in the mind of another,
 Is recipient of such varied reactions
 For no reason other than the nature
 Of the early, developmental, years.
This is how it can be that all men deserve freedom.
I have heard it said, certain freedom are undeserved;
But this is absolutely not so!
 One cannot be made to *think;*
  So one must have the *freedom* to do so.
 Hand-in-hand with which is freedom to feel,
  Whether those feelings grate against others';
 And the freedom to express our thoughts and feelings
  Yes, these are three basic freedoms.
But if a good man does not murder,
 Yet another man does so kill,
 And the first man fears,
 —Is the first man to live afraid?
 Or may he purchase a weapon for possible defense?
 And even if he is never attacked,
 His fear is part of his child's environment,
 Such that his children fear, also—

And shall seek to protect themselves;
        There can be no grandfather clause.
Neither can one generation possess,
        But not another—
                For that might as well be the same thing.
Not only should he protect from fellow man,
But also him and his family,
Should it come to that,
                                from malicious government.
After all:
Should man be allowed to think, speak, and act,
Not as he is told but as he wishes;—
Surely some things will be done and said,
Politically, which in the past have stirred the anger
—Even the wrath, it can be said—
Of those in position of power.
That is the importance of political balance:
        First and foremost each person is a human,
                Who by merit of birth, has the right to life
                (But who, by merit of conception, does not necessarily)
        Therefore friend and enemy alike should be treated
        At all times, as such;
                                That is, as a *human being*.
Second comes each person's freedom to think,
        To speak, and to act; which, being free,
        Is linked inextricably with privacy:
        By the individual as well as by government,
        Individual privacy must be respected,
        Even unto a prerequisite Mandate
        That allows entry with or without permission
        In order to conduct the specific act(s) so necessary:
        For why do you insist upon entrance?

In order to know my thoughts,
Do you pry my brain from my skull?
What is it you seek?
        What so demands your entrance?
        —Only a search for criminal evidence
        Is so pertinent and necessary;
        And even then—what do you seek,
        Where do you expect you'll find it,
        And what purpose serves this search and seizure?
Should you find what you seek,
I have not to confess to anything:
        Why should I indict myself?
        I am free to do as I please—
        (So long as I don't get caught!)
And that includes not confessing,
        Since the choice *not to,*
        Is just as much a choice *to.*
Yea, I say gather your evidence,
        Take me to trial,
        Give me a lawyer so I have a chance,
        Treat me well by keeping me informed
                Of accusations, progress, and setbacks;
                And by torturing me not,
                Since I am allowed to maintain silence.
Further I say *take* me to trial,
        But if you fail to convict me,
        That's too bad—you had your chance.
Indeed, let me sit in on my trial;
Allow me to witness my accuser;
And allow me to defend myself!
For I am a human,
                Free to think, speak, act of my will,

Accordingly,
    Within the law,
        Yet simultaneously as I see fit.
Therefore I must be allowed my defense—
    For *you* would seek it, too;
And I ask of men,
    No more than I expect them to ask of me.
At all times I should have the option of jury—
    Of nonbiased opinion.
—Ah!
But now you say you find fault?
In what?
    In that a jury of *peers* does not exist?
    Do you really think that true?
—For you are right.
Absolutely and without a doubt,
                        All men are created unequal;
And at once,
All men are endowed at birth with those various basic rights.
Men must be treated equally,
    Not as if all are the same.
It may happen that certain of a particular hue
Prove more suited to athletics
    Or to innovation;
    To family;
        Or to business;
    To medicine,
    To law,
    To science,
        Or to the arts.
But as often as a stereotype is fulfilled,
    It faces retaliation.

All men deserve equal opportunity,
    But not equal involvement.
    If the skinny geek should stick to books,
    Don't force him to join the team!
    If the same child really persists,
    Encourage the persistence,
        Without really molding the direction.
It's okay to be insufficient
                in certain areas: for,
Knowing our limits,
        We begin to know ourselves.
Everything exists of its own accord,
In its own realm, where it is individual;
Possessing, generally, certain rights
    (Much more applicable to reasoning creatures than
anything else,
    But also, in a reasonable way, to non-reasoning plants,
    Animals, and Earth, as well),
Which ensure the freedom of Self
Against the tyranny of others;
    Of the laws,
        Of government,
            Of the fellow man.

# *Religion*

Recognizing which, it must be said,
That if we are free to think
                              Then we are free to believe;
Not, that is, in the prescribed doctrine,
    But in any doctrine—or none—of our own choosing.
Yet, there is much to be said of religion, so-called,
Not the least of which
    Are the similarities shared in each and every.


Watch the sun.
It moves across the sky.
Perfectly,
               or at least close enough.
…The light feeds the grass,
    The grass feeds the animal,
        The animal feeds the man.
Everything is a conversion
    Of light into energy;
        Energy is
            Mass times the speed of light squared.
If God is All,
                   is in Everything,
Then God is Light, and Time, and Energy, and Matter;
    Is in me and you and this and that.
God—
        —is the sun!
Generally we tell stories,
    For that is how we explain what we see:
    God the sun rises only so high
                  at certain times of year;

God must be losing the battle.
Lo!
      Behold the cross-pattern of stars in the sky!
      Mark the time:
                        'Tis December.
Watch!
      —As the sun sinks lower!
            Will God die?
                        What is the date?
            God followed the trunk of the cross,
                  God died on the cross!
                              —'Tis December twenty-second.
Look!
      The sun stays! ;
Lo!
      The sun rises
            after it was dead three days!
Three?
      Yes; today is the twenty-third.
      Watch the sky, wait for the sign:
      The Eastern star shall shine,
      And the three that follow it
            —These are the three kings,
                                    Or Orion's belt
—Which "announce" the "birth" of the God!
(But on what day is God born?)
Re-born, re-born!
                        —on the twenty-fifth.
      Watch: You'll see.
      The sun followed the stem of the cross,
      Reaching a very low point in the sky;
            And our people said God was dead,

And evil was to overtake us all.
Yet God never disappeared and,
On the third day,
The sun rose;
And will rise,
From the twenty-fifth unto the equinox,
Which is when we celebrate
God's full resurrection;
And God, being so pleased,
Causes the earth to be plentiful.
This is winter; this is spring.
In summer the God(s) [is-slash-are] most
fierce,
For we, so joyous and celebratory,
Always live in excess insofar as we're capable;
And after three months' penance
God relents…
Only to be thereby and again
Defeated by the evil force, the passive principle.
Which is why God's presence is most felt in the desert.

God always returns, why? —Because God is the *sun*-ah!
God is accompanied, in the stories,
By twelves,
For the signs in the stars.
…Moses defeated the golden calf
Because it represented Taurus, the bull;
The old age, astrologically,
While Moses was the ram, Aries,
Representing the new age;
And Jesus and the New Testament
Makes much reference to "fish"

Partly in relation to Jesus'
Being symbolic of Pisces,
    Of the new age,
        Come to replace Moses' old;
Which explains why,
    At the end of *this* age,
    There shall come
        "The man carrying water",
This being the new age of Aquarius.


That in the by-and-by,
Whence came Jesus?
                        Of a virgin named Mary?

Why, yes, of course:
                That is what is said, after all.
But oh, the context.
Mary was a nun.
                Nuns were called  *virgins*.
Joseph was a priest
    Married to a nun Mary named,
        Called in society
                An "embodiment of the *holy spirit*":
And so it was that the *virgin* Mary
Conceived by the *holy spirit*.
                        …Where were they?
In a little village run the Essenes,
Extremely orthodox folk by that well-known Sea.
And of the mythology surrounding Jesus' birth
I have already spoken: For
    God—
                —is the sun!
The sun—Jesus—rose December twenty-fifth,

Birth having been announced by the Eastern star
    And "three kings", or Orion's belt;
At Easter is celebrated the resurrection,
Which followed three days' "death"
    On the "cross" (of stars).
                        Ha-ha, la-di-dah, lazy-daisy-yay!
It's amazing what can be thought.
When the mind is used for thinking.
                                …Ah;
                                    "But what,"
                                        You ask,
"Of all Jesus' miracles?";
                        And I say, "What of them?
Wine was once served to the 'upper class,'
    To those of the priesthood;
        To those at the high table(s),
            Within the temple.
Those without, drank water:
            But Jesus gave them the key to the cellar.
…At his death Jesus bled,
    Something he could do only if he was alive
                                (for Jesus *was* a
man, after all);
The letting was a test to be sure of life,
For the bitter drink previously administered
Was bitter for the presence of poison.
Appearing dead, then,
He was taken down and away,
    And later retrieved,
        Administered a remedy so as to live,
(In which absence, of course his grave was empty)
Nursed back to health

To make an appearance after three days' "death".
(Then what?)
—Some say he ran off to France,
The "holy grail" being Jesus' unborn child,
Growing inside Mary and born there,
Jesus being, in the end,
    The founder of a line of French kings
    Which may or may not have died off;
        But the continued existence of which,
        Kept secret or forgotten, is understandable,
    Considering the supposed continued existence of David's
line at the time of Jesus' birth.
After all,
    Some new Christ—see "messiah"—
    Will come along,
    At the appropriate time or not;
    Whether it is true or not.
        The age will end,
            A new one will begin.
The truth of this;
    The predictability—
        Unknown variables
            Tainted—
                Helped—
                    Touched, in any case,
                        By unforeseen factors.


    …And the various miracles can be explained,
Rationally, should one choose to do so.
Or one may believe the myth:
    The Devil,
        Or Absolute Evil,

May or may not exist;
God, as man defines God,
    Is in the same predicament.
Faced with so many interpretations of a single religion as
Christianity,
One must acknowledge its factions
Represent the pagan bases of its so-called monotheism.
    Yet,
Christianity's theft and disfigurement of past pagan religion(s)
Is only slightly more evident than Moses' own same.
    The myth of his birth, for example,
        Was stolen almost word-for word
            From (a) past religion(s);
As was the tale of Noah and his ark,
And Joseph's tale is, at bottom,
    No more than elaborated history.
The various miracles,
Dreams, occurrences, and so on,
Are acknowledged as being symbolic
    As well as historical.
And while, furthermore,
    The Old may be discredited
        As easily as the New,
Nothing has killed more than the mandate to:
Take over the world by talking it out.
In the historical of the Old,
War happens and the good guys win;
Law is established accordingly;
History is recorded with, simply,
A religious bent.
                    (Mohammed was a desperate man.)
Knowing what there is to be known,

The Jews deserve all of Israel,
The Christians have exactly no claim to fame.
The Muslims should just write a law book,
      And form a government,
            In which God has no part.
The various morals of all
Should be de-mystified
      And re-philosophized
And recorded in a big Book of Morals,
      Adherence to which is voluntary.
Of other religion there is little to say.
Many peoples are peaceable;
As much war is Economical
      As religious-based, give or take.
Criticism of religion, in any case,
Is permissible but not enforceable,
Since we are free—
      Oh so free! to think, to act, to speak, to believe.
As when government is oppressive we must fight back,
So too with the power and control
      Wielded, represented, by religion.

## *A Number of Things*

It can be said I'm a simple man,
But I'm not a simpleton.
Hailing from the sticks, which
Hold together adobe bricks,
Am I an inextricable part of structure?
Be that the source of my simplicity?
For indeed: Being with so many,
Realizing the futility of competition,
I am compelled to merely exist.
    I am invited to do, but not to think;
    I am told to join,
              Yet turned away at first signs of enthusiasm.
What is the point of freedom?
Does my individuality make me happy,
Or you because you haven't to worry of me?
Does my uniquity bind my Self with others,
Or does it push them away?
They are in total contradiction,
Individuality and Freedom;
Perpendicular to Group and Obligation.
; …And these are the four points of reason.
We can only be free if we can think;
But why think if others will do it for us?
…Does Nature proceed blindly,
    Attaining perfection by accident,
    Or does It work in tandem with itself,
    As does the human brain and body?
What—Where—is Nature's brain?
What are we?
           We are the brain.

Think of yourself as the world:
A majority of fluid,
With a little solid surface;
Everything about us quite unthinking,
Except the brain but variously motivated by
        The reproductive organs,
            And the immune system.
Obviously the latter is the legislative force,
The brain is both executive and judicial,
Those organs being militant.
In another sense, the brain is humanity,
The immune system is animal,
And the organs Nature Itself.
—So what is the purpose of our brains?
To reason, to think to—to what?
It is, however "pointless", here to stay…
But why?
Wrap your mind around it, man!
    Why?!
To raise a fam'ly? —No.
To chase some dream? —No.
To procreate? —No.
    …Yet, *yes* to all of these:
    For they, being done,
Required the consumption, transformation, and expulsion of
energy;
    And that is the ultimate process,
    The basis of all things.
From whence came the energy,
    The initial consumption thereof,
    Its transformation
    And all subsequent expulsion and repetition?

Why does the energy exist, and where?
How? —Is it Light? It is sucrose?
Is it the so-called Spark of Life?
Who is it, if it is anybody?
    (If it *is* anybody, it is-are [the] God[s].)
There are those who might claim, wrongly,
God is the answer of those too lazy;
Too lazy to think, to consider; too.
But I say the case is exactly opposite:
One *must* think, so much it troubles,
Unto exhaustion, of all possibilities;
And ultimately come to draw a blank.
Whence came the first action?
    There is no, nor will there ever be any, way to know.
    In the mind, therefore,
      "God" is the answer,
    Whatever the idol that symbolizes.
God is both male and female,
    Because who knows which came first?
God is parental because *we* come from *ours,*
    And all-knowing because we perceive them as such;
    Yet as we age, we realize of them:
    That we are as old as them,
      And we know what we know,
    Which means they knew about the same.
      —Therefore the God(s) [has/have] a plan.
Why wouldn't God?
    Of course, we cannot understand that plan,
    Same as we cannot fathom God's origin,
    —Not, that is, in an individual, free society:
    For in such monotheism must predominate:
      Knowing humans are fickle,

And that parents are like us
Why go to any but the source?
Certainly God delegates,
But that's God's prerogative,
Same as it's mine to go to God,
                              Directly or in-.
So everything comes from God,
Who knows and has plans for everything;
And we're part of that plan,
     But we cannot ever fully understand it,
     Because we haven't the God-view,
     Which is amalgamation of all possibilities.
     The closest we can get, for understanding,
     Is to refer back to the four points of reason,
          Individual, freedom, group, and obligation.
And generally the closest we can get to comprehension
Is consideration and-slash-or implementation
Of the US Constitution, the Bill of Rights, and Capitalism.
…We are the brain, yes?
I don't always know:
Should I take a drug,
     My mind knows but not my body.
Likewise humans' treatment of Earth.
Brain and body work in tandem,
As Humans and Nature do,
Aware but unaware of
     —Individual and separate from—
          The other(s);
Even as we are part of a larger system.
As is the blood cell to humans' eyes,
     So are humans in God's eye.
*But,*

Do we have a *plan* for that blood cell?
Or do we know its purpose,
        Its *expected* course of "action"?
And when something goes wrong, what?
        What then?
Trial and error.
        *There's* a motto for the masses.
        (Certainly it is God's).
Well, God is all-knowing,
        And has a plan,
            It might be said;
But I shan't even dignify with response.
And again it must be asked,
        "What is the point?
        What
          is
        the
            f
                u
                    c
                        k
                            i
                                n
                                    g
point?
Why shouldn't I give in to excess?
I can do what I want, and when.
You don't really care about me,
        Except as it makes you look socially.
And I certainly don't care about you.
The only reasons I don't commit murder
Are that I don't want to go to jail,

And if reality is a projection of myself,
	Then any death incurred by myself is basically a form of
suicide.
Yet, this is only possible in a civil society.
Indeed, that is the difference
	Between past and modern man:
Today we do as we please, no matter;
But maintain civility to continue doing so.
Not even medieval noblemen were so proper.
…Still, "death is change."
As death begets new life,
	So life begets all death;
As capitalism begets Marxism and such,
	So		communism		(a		sophisticated
feudal		society)		leads		to		capitalism.
Often viewed as a struggle for dominance,
The ideal of one ruling forevermore
	Is a strictly political ideal,
		Never to be actually attained
	But only to spur enthusiasm for one's cause;
Because the two extremes must exist.
	"Death is change." Without it, what is there?
	Just imagine eternal life for all,
	The ideal of so many:
Were we to exist as they wish, nothing would change.
With no death war is eliminated by default;
Since there's no war there's negotiation;
Since we talk out our problems,
	There's no anger;
		No pride;
		No envy.
				…Perfect, right?

But then nothing changes,
Unto the point that time stops,
    The earth stands still,
        The sun is neither hot nor cold,
            Neither light not dark.
That, my friend, is nothingness.
Imagine walking up, even in, to the sun.
    That is nothingness,
    That is eternal life,
    That is eternity;
*But that is not life after death:*
In absolutely no deniable way,
We live eternally by nourishing the soil,
In which crawls that worm;
From which sprouts all vegetation,
Which feeds all life in the cycle,
Unto the point of death equaling energy equaling life,
Equaling energy equaling death.
So why not give in to excess?
    —Again, it has to do with the First Knowledge,
    And subsequent perceptions,
    And the base operation of the consciousness as receptionist.


…Sex for pleasure is a necessity.
Observe those both with and without it;
    Strange, yes?
Likewise all inebriation,
Whichever way we escape:
Alcohol, music, love, drugs, sex, art.
Observe those stark-sober, surrounding you.
    Me.        Us.

Reality is a conscious creation,
As it requires a perceivably logical order
     To be defined as such.
I look through my eyes through your eyes;
Through which I perceive myself
Even as you are my conscious creation
Perceived by my Self as
     I look through my eyes through your eyes.


Madness mirrors our Selves,
Effectively re-dis-establishing all we thought we knew,
Off'ring glimpse at perception unchecked,
Reinforchecking the pompousness of sanity
Even as others perceive us in the same way we do them,
So that we must ask ourselves what we know
And admit we know nothing,
     But assume, presume, reason, conclude, reconsider.


What, then, of history, past, memory?
History is the collective recollection
     Of collective perception of the collective self.
Individually the same is true;
All things being perceived,
     And therefore a realization of self,
Even memory, past, and such are perceptions
Of perceptions of your self,
Unto the nonexistence of past or future
But only the present—
          Past and future, and memory and environment,
          Being relative perceptions of realizations of self,
          Such that I live, I am present, I exist.
     Constantly things change,

But change is relative,

Because there is only change in the over-all perception,

Which acts to continually affirm one's existence by sensation,

Perception of "change" "in" "how" "one" "felt" "or" "existed" "before".

History is perception of the greater, "universal," God-Self.

# *Idolatry*

A problem is that we tend to idolize.
    Which makes sense:
        If history is a realization of the God-Self,
        And all reality is pretty much the same,
            Why *wouldn't we idolize?*
                    —Deal with it.


…The question is *how.*

                      How to deal with it?
Well, why—and what—do we idolize?
    —Power, money, fame;
        …Family, freedom, solitude.
Allow some simple imagination:
    The strong survive.
A little power is good.
    A comfortable quantity of "wealth", is good.
        A bit of repu*ta*tion is good.
And those later three are,
    Simply,
            Absolutes.
Yet we idolize unknowable things,
That we may better know them;
                *(God—*
                    —*is the sun!)*
This being true not only of God(s),
But of good crops
    And the techniques employed;
Good genes
    And the offspring produced:
Successful systems, generally,

And their resultant productivity.
…Yet power is all too often abused,
Money's worth is debatable,
Fame can only last so long;
    And all three must be renounced
        In order for a proper family;
    Whereas freedom can be had either way,
    And solitude the same.
Accompanying all three are:
    The seven deadly sins, so-called:
    Greed, lust, gluttony, sloth,
    Envy, wrath, and pride.
…But to what degree?
How much greedier the businessman,
    Who harvests fruits of labor
        *From* the labor of his workers,
Than the farmer,
    Who harvests fruits of labor
        Requiring human as well as earthen labor?
Philosophically they are not different,
All differences being checked by exemption.
What be the level of lust to be seen
In a whore, a housewife, a man, a priest?
    Sex happens, whether or not for reproduction;
        And relatively often:
            For the mandate to populate is,
                        to say the least,
        Just another excuse for men to demand.
Gluttony is another form of greed,
    Both resulting from:
        Hurt pride,
        And resultant wrath or envy,

                                        or both.
But is the man of the middle class
     Apt to be more openly proud of his accomplishment,
Bringing attention,
     And both praise and criticism,
     To the product of his hard labor
—Than, on the other hand,
A business-type who, also proud,
     Does nothing much different?
When slighted, is greater wrath felt
                         By this man as opposed to that one?
     Tempers flare, anger is unavoidable at times.
     As with all things
          Individual perception plays a large part,
          But a spade is a spade,
               Black is black
                    Open is open
                         And so on and so forth.
Envy is learned still very young,
When we want what *she* had, Mommy-uh!
We connive to obtain, then,
     And either fail or succeed,
But either way continue to do so the whole of our lives.
The real sin is experiencing any of the above
And doing nothing to fix the problem,
                              so perceived.
     …Yet, to check the vices,
               One must be careful not to go extreme:
The "holy" virtues
     (Chastity, abstinence, temperance,
     Diligence patience, kindness, humility)
Must be exercised

—and wielded
            —with great caution.
The question of moderation is one with answer
As wide-ranging as a moment's definition.
For some, any of either is too much
                        —But even this is extreme,
                            Inadvisable;
(and obvious).
For most, a little of each is acceptable,
    Citing the symbolic yin-yang as example.
Then again, how much is enough?
Are there equal portions of each, vice and virtue,
    Or is there more of one than another?
        —Can humanity so conform?
In answer, it is good to say:
    "I am who I am."
The amount of this or that vice or virtue
    To be found in an individual
    Has much to do with the First Knowledge
    And the individuality of the individual.
    Neither should be judged:
    For when it comes down to the line,
    Only the uneducated
        Are truly capable of hate;
    While the partially educated
        Will tend to dislike;
    And the proper-educated,
        Will tend to just deal.


Now, the philosophy by which one man lives
*Should* not be exactly the same as another's;
But all men should take time to consider,

Thoroughly, the other point of view.
    Otherwise we shall idolize:
Virtues found in this or that are profound,
Are examined, argued, debated,
Contorted, discarded, left to decay
    In the minds of the disciples
    Who receive fractions
                        of the original message.
Otherwise, we shall idolize.
Who are the idols?
The leaders,
    The heads,
        The foremost of the *Group.*
Individuals do not idolize, *per se,* but love;
    Idolizing only if the thing was lost.
Why the sun?
    Because we "almost lost it"
    When it lay "dead" for three days.
Why this or that person?
    Because s/he exhibits those qualities,
    Virtues, philosophies, and such,
That one holds dear;
    *Which* are held dear for the First Knowledge.
Thus as individuals we do idolize,
Since face-to-face we do not fawn,
                        but converse,


or act.
Yet our idolatry is for a fear
Of that which we hold dear, or love.
As we meet others of similar mold,
We tend to befriend them and, together,

Start a *group.*

A *group,* is that formed by two or more like-minded,
conscious,
entities.
Being a member of such as,
One cannot help but be affected by,

                              nor but to affect,
                other members thereof.
Groups are shaped by ideals.
These, originally, are individual ideals
                    based on First Knowledge and so on,
Which we share with each other in the course of things.
Yet once there is agreement between two or more,
There are now two—*three*—layers of perception:
    Of the first $(-1 \times -1 = 1)$,
        Of the second $(0 + 1 = 1)$,
            And the two $(1 + 1 = 2)$.
The percept- of the two is desirable and usually chosen.
In the course of things,
    Individual acts, quips, occurrences,
    Are telling, informing the other(s)
    Of true emotion(s) and thought(s);
        Which will evolve,
Though whether into the group's,
    Or further into one's, ideal(s),
is debatable.
The result, is one of two:
    Grow closer, drift apart.
Indeed:
    The *group,* when first formed,
    Is easily manageable,
        (And often progresses no further than)

But at length the mass becomes as much,
And a sculptor is the logical solution.
        Thus, a leader *be* chosen,
        Who is a representative
        Of the group's various ideals,
        And whose main concern is order,
Gen'rally maintained
By maintaining the majority,
    The status quo,
        The ideal.
It is, they are,
The means by which this is done,
That gains the leaders
                        (and subordinates),
Or causes for the loss of, favor.
Either way, the ideal is subsequently altered,
On both the group and individual levels.
In the case of a loss of favor, however,
The individual opinion shines through:
A second group is thus formed,
And both, from that point onward,
Put up with each other face-to-face,
Then gnash teeth when backs are turned.
Now the layers of perception are more:
Being of the individual,
The second individual,
                and the group, initially;
Then being of the first individual within,
The sub-group, and
    (amidst the starting of the process)
Either growing closer or distant.
…Such is the result of idolatry.

Unifying fractionalism.
Such are all things.
What is *not* a part of a group, or chain?
What does *not* feel effect from,
        Or offer anything to, that group?
Who has no individual opinion
Aside from those fanatics and extremists who,
Thinking not for themselves,
                    Are not really alive, anyway?
In the setting of a work environment,
Which colleagues do you befriend,
Which do you put up with,
        Which do you simply not like?
In the setting of a home environment,
The fam'ly unit itself is the prime example.
And politically and religiously,
We've only to hit the books for a play-by-play.
It is the phenomenal result
        Of the freedom to think
            And all that that entails,
Checked by the slavery of others' freedom.
(For we are enslaved to others' freedom,
As much me to you as you to me)
        Yea, this is idolatry.
The result of it.
(A consequence?)
Emotions become our idols
The group opinion becomes our idol;
The ideal is the extreme;
And all contained hereby:
        The strong survive,
                    but the meek shall inherit the earth.

# *Language*

At the base of all problems
    Lies mis- or non-communication.
The obvious solution is to quit stupefying our children.
Throw your television(s) away!
Forget about the new techno-gadget!
Why can't we slow down to write a letter?
    We move *too fast* for electronic mail?
So busy we must "text" each other,
    Unto the point of writing whole books
    In the "language" thereof, so-called.
    There's the thing, though:
        We're too busy for *any*thing.
That upon which we choose to focus
    (for the moment)
Is only in passing.
This or that doesn't really matter,
In the whole spectrum.
    *That* is the view of all others.
To the individual,
    The cause and effect of happiness
        Is as varied as the stars.
I really don't care who is or was "that guy,"
    If it has to do with sports
        Or media,
                for example;
But speak to me of White House secrets,
    Conspiracy theories, general politics,
    Rock 'n' roll—then you have my attention.
Yet in all cases, a proper language is needed.
Whatever that language be,

It should not be abbreviated;
For this leads to miscommunication.
How are we to act
        If you won't say what you mean?
Our knowledge of the ancient past is spotty
Why?
—Partly because their written communication was pictorial,
        A shortened version of the language itself,
        Whereby five scholars may draw five different conclusions,
        All from the same piece.
English is one of the superior languages,
Not for beauty of phonetics
But variety of word
        And ability to specify.
Where are you coming from?
        Where are you going?
                —Both have to do with where you are.
        What is your point?
What is your plan?
Specify, be specific:
        Ask for what you want,
                Do not beat around a shrubbery!
        Say what you mean to say:
                Do not turn to imaginative,
colorful language of the Passive-Aggressive.
        Do as you intend,
        Do as you please,
                Without worry of damn consequence!
And when questioned,
                        *Specify!*


It is curious some teach, "think before you speak";

For those so taught, are always thinking.
What conclusion may be drawn,
When the process is incomplete?
     —The proper instruction is:
     "Think before you speak;
     Say what you think;
     Mean what you say."
If we do all these,
     Rather than merely the first,
Then honesty—with self, then other(s)—
     Is prerequisite,
As well as a relative mastery of the native tongue.
And a willingness to act:
     For when in doubt,
          "Communication
                    Is the first step to solution."
     Meaning communication *is* action.
In a free society,
     The non-voter deserves no specific treatment.
S/He deserves those rights naturally belonging thereto,
But as far as government goes,
     Nothing can be said,
          Because the opportunity was not taken
          To change, fix, improve,
          When opportunity was presented.
Likewise the silent witness
     Who is an accessory to murder,
     Or theft, or rape, or crime in general.
…Let it merely be kept in mind:
You haven't to be *correct,*
                         just vocal.
Do not say what is not meant,

For what is the point?
In a free society
The only true prison is one's mind:
Throw me in a jail cell,
     And I can still think.
To take *that* from me,
I'll require seducing.
In a free society,
     Individual freedom must be clearly communicated:
     I am free to think, first and foremost,
     And, therefore, to act and speak the same.
     However you possess the same rights,
     So that
          Neither has right to the other's life,
          Neither has right to dominate,
               In any way, shape, or form,
               Assuming the domination
                    Is not sexual
                    Or mutually agreed upon.
(For in a free society, those in power are there for a mutual or
majority agreement of the people.)
     Of course you cannot rape others, then,
          Neither physically nor otherwise.
     And possessions?
     Those are earned, to be treasured.
     …To steal—
                         O!—
Not only is it a grave ignorance,
     A severe breach of privacy,
     But also it is a statement:
          Are you the non-voter?
He who does not vote in a free society

Is as good as a thief,
Stealing for himself extraneous rights,
    Which are part of the national laws
    To which all citizens are subject,
    And by which all are likewise protected.
Such is one form of theft,
one "statement" to make.
What shines through, always
    —The statement of every single crime—
Is, *I am not whole.*
                        And why aren't you?
Because your daddy hit you?
Because your grammaw touched you?
Because daddy hit mommy?
Because one of your parents is dead?
                        …But these answers matter not.
                        Not generally:
For the answer to that question,
    "What makes me incomplete?"
    Is definitive of one's First Knowledge,
    Relative to one's passion and motivation,
    And ultimately subject to change
        As we learn more about ourselves
        And our surrounding environment(s).
But your crime *is* a cry for help;
For which you may be pitied
    And, when apprehended, subject to due process;
    Even unto assuming innocence 'til it's proven otherwise,
Even as you are punished accordingly when found guilty.
For in a free society
    There is no tolerance of crime,
        Not on any level or in any way,

But accurate, appropriate punishment in case of.
You commit your crime
        As a means to cry for help,
                Due to your lack of completeness.
Yet I too, am incomplete!
        Why don't I lie?
        Why don't I not vote?
        Why don't I take others' possessions?
                For morals? —Bah!
                                        Morals are relative.
                For a sense of completeness.
                        My insecurity is less than yours.
Begging, then, to know who deserves higher praise:
Me, for being just oh so good,
Or you, for soldiering on in spite of everything?
Or both, for our various attributes,
        Ridiculed for detractive features.
…It's *all* relative.
I am as free as you,
        And of course you as me;
Subject to all that you are;
The only individual trait
        I truly possess
                Being that of the First Knowledge,
                My subsequent perceptions,
And my only means of participating
—Of contributing to the general history
—Is by communicating,
        Through beautiful,
                Unabbreviated if at times somewhat grammatically
incorrect,

Language.
Were I to think of what to say,
    Then say what I'd thought,
        Meaning what I had said,
            Whether or not I might be right,
                Which forces an honesty,
                    That   disallows   for   negative
emotion,
Perhaps you would return the "favor" and,
With us, the whole of society.
If we said what we meant,
    There'd be no need of jealousy:
        Because you know that s/he said what s/he said,
        And that s/he meant it.
    Neither a need of greed:
*Motivation,* yes;
        But with honesty prevalent
                        —The Honest Standard—
                Honesty and the slave-driver of freedom
                    And clear communication,
        Motivation might be the greatest extent of greed.
There are two problems with pure honesty, however, and they
are:
        That honest people are gullible by default,
        And the whole of mankind cannot be made to be honest,
            Except in the case of extermination of all but a fraction
of one per cent thereof.
And secondly,
That we do not fully comprehend language.
When I say, "Mean what you say,"
I mean: Know what you're saying with each word;

Be aware of the context in which your case or argument is
presented,
And imagine the response(s) you will receive,
    And your response(s) to their response(s).
When you use a certain word,
    Do you mean it as Webster defines it,
    Or in another context of your own coloring?
When you structure your sentence,
    Is it well-presented?
    The answer is had by writing.
        Write as you talk and think;
        Compare to the writing in a book;
        And find a medium.
                It is in this way reading improves writing,
                And writing language,
                And language society.
…Our perception of the world
Is defined by the level of mastery of one's language.
In a society with abbreviated language,
We have citizens with abbreviated thoughts;
And these are those who feel incomplete.
Throw in an abbreviated education,
Abbreviated education of religion(s),
Abbreviation through profitously capitalist distractions,
    Of political and social awareness,
Abbreviation of the family unit,
Abbreviation of tradition—
                        And,
                                Fucking A,
                                    *There* ya go,
                                        *T h a t 's*
America.

Are you happy?
Are you happy?
Ask yourself:
                    Are you fucking happy?
Why do we continue to live in this misinformed,
miscommunicated, miseducated, misnomer of society?
Because the hippies are running things, so to speak? Well they
had *their* revolution, do with it as they may; now we have
ours!
    Is it such a radically new consciousness,
                                        T   h   e

Honest Standard?
We can be honest,
    As long as we are aware
        That some people are dishonest.
Keep an eye out for those people.
    But sometimes shit fucking happens, man;
        So fucking what.
That is *no* excuse to be dishonest,
By which I mean incommunicative,
Non-committal, non-participatory.
When you lose a loved one you may feel incomplete—
But if you *talk* about it, something will happen.
Whether it's good or bad is up to your perceptions;
    But something happens.
Yet it can *only* happen if we are honest.
    Communicative.
        Respectful of our language,
        The things we have done with it,
        Those things it can help us do in the future.

# *Standard*

What, then, is the standard?
Here we exist, as individual Conscious Beings,
Generally relative to environment,
Capable of reasoning, logical thinking,
Communication through superb language(s),
Free to do pretty much as we please,
    So long as we're honest and aware,
Without need of specific religion,
    But well-rounded in myth and non-myth,
    Since it is important to understand
    That which has dominated mankind
    Through the whole of its existence.
To know the standard,
    We must return to the *group;*
    And as we've already discussed that,
    The quasi-existent moral standard(s) created by them.


There are political ideals, yes;
    But the only one to be considered,
    And which has generally been,
    Is that of the free society.
    That is a group and group philosophy
    In which all mankind
        Should have a chance to participate
There are personal ideals,
    Results of and defined by
        Perceptions and the First Knowledge.
And then there are group ideals,
Which if they are not political
    They are moral;

And the moral is no more than the prevailing sense,
    Within that group,
  Of what is right and what is wrong.
Inescapable, however, are one's family's values,
    Which forever affect our sense of right, wrong, excess,
conservation, good, bad, and so on, whether for better or for
worse.


There are those with mandate to honor:
    God, Mother, Father, Fellow-Man,
    Country, Neighbor, Leader, and so on.
…Some may live honoring all of these quite consciously,
While others live acknowledging much but honoring few.
Either way, it is important,
Especially as children but throughout life, as well,
To have an authority, a leader,
    To accept as well as dish out
      Both praise and criticism.
  And if I am the leader,
    Then past is precedent,
        Freedom prevalent,
            Action in the name thereof.
For indeed:
  Should I ignore the past,
    I then ignore origin,
        I ignore my various perceptions of Self,
            Which is where so many things begin.
  Should I render freedom illegal,
    Then's when I've begun my tyranny,
    Though of course the leader's goal is to unite.


The standard's origin lies in the First Knowledge,

And any and all subsequent perceptions.
Nothing prevents me from this or that,
Save my sense of right, wrong, and so on,
　　Which is a direct result thereof
　　　　And relative to environment.
Honor is adhering to the Honest Standard;
Respect is the result of honor well-worn.
…*Joining* the group is not the problem
(But lack of communication therewithin),
　　　　　　　In a sense of "naturalness",
Because we are born into them,
　　　　　　　　　In the form of family
units,
　　　　　　　　Whence comes our First
Knowledge.
As we age, the Honest Standard of Mum an' Da'
Are learned and known and prevalent.
　　Our individual knowledge(s),
　　Come(s) from everyday observation(s),
　　Tempered by mastery of language
　　　　　　　　　　(and use of it),
　　Which affects understanding of all things.
The self-discipline resultant thereof
　　Is the individual moral,
　　Which if it is a tourist attraction
　　　　Is less popular than the Honest Standard;
　　And, in fact,
　　Is also less popular than the group ideal;
　　But *certainly* no less important.
Indeed,
　　　　　Its importance cannot be emphasized
enough.

# *Epilogue*

Considering these things,
    Various questions do certainly arise
    Ranging from the abortion issue
                (What is the value of life in a perfectly
individual society,
        And what is it if you are everything and I am everything,
too?)
    To a proper method of food preparation
    To war and marriage and the desirability of capitalism.
In fact, the former pair are juxtapositional:
We plant the seed,
    Grow the plant,
        Harvest the nourishing substance(s),
            Cook [it/them]
And at this point we consume it;
And have the right to like or dislike;
                Even to discard of it;
Even
    To save the leftovers,
        Which may or may not be put to further, future, use.
Almost the same is true of fetuses
    Not the cooking and eating,
    But the planting, the growing,
        The throwing away,
    Even the leftovers saved.
Animals kill their offspring, yes,
    *For lack of suitability to substantial life;*
    Such that in humans,
        This instinct must also exist.

What of war, then?
    War is economical.
In a capitalist society,
    It is necessary.
Capitalism,
it is said,
Is the only economic ideal suitable to a free society.
…Personally, I fancy a garden, a farm,
                              Self-sufficiency;
                        But not for everyone,
                  And even if for, only temporarily.
No; for everyone, capitalism.
    Why?
        Because it *is* the only proper ideal.
If I want to market this or that product or service,
I can,
    And I will.
You may want to do the same thing,
    And we'll compete.
        One wins,
            One loses,
                But who and who?
                    …Does it really matter?
        I think not.
*But*…
    *But.*
If we all had access to a farm…
Well, we wouldn't need much else,
    Because we'd have it all.
Yet in the garden or fields would we always find ourselves,
Even unto feuds with otherwise fellow neighbors;
    And how can we quite progress from there?

See, I want my produce and meat from market;
     It's fun to do-it-yourself,
But only because it's all right if I fail;
And this is somewhat why supermarkets are so prevalent,
     And why a so-called "return" to Nature is a *progression*.
Food ready-grown, pre-packaged
Oh, what? Pre-made meals!
                    No, no, no.
Fake soil leads to fake plants to fake feed
     To fake animals to fake humans.
The only way to attain the ideal
     Is to institute it so that *it* is the standard,
     Even as that is a contradiction of its own terms,
     Both from and to which citizens may run.
In general, the government, which attempts to adhere to the
ideal,
At the head; and, separately, little socio-anarchic communes,
     Which are small-scale versions of the greater whole.
     If the parts adhere to the ideal,
          Then the rest should follow.
Within the commune,
     There is a certain quantity of land;
A percentage of which is managed by the community—
     By those who *desire* to do so,
          And express their desire
          In campaigning for election to a sort of care-taking
position.
Elsewise, all land is divided amongst the citizens,
All portions initially equal except in cases of mutual agreement,
But the elected officials would not own their own land while
in office.
Rather, they would live much as the preacher does,

Provided for not by church but community.
Each participant would build their own shelter,
    At least in the sense that the whole community
        Would have to build the whole community:
    For if one person's influence is predominant,
        Then the ideal has already been lost.
    Should the community build itself,
    No individual will be prone to feeling a sense of property,
    Which is necessary, considering the commune is
temporary;
Whereas in the greater scheme of things,
    Each would own private property
    And be allowed to acquire more as needed or capable.
The best parts of the land should be used for farming.
    Ideally, all parts of land would be the best parts,
    And everyone would do a little of their own farming,
        But that is not necessarily likely to be the case,
        Depending on where the commune is located.
        Lacking fertile soil, the ideal is already defeated,
            Except insofar as:
                Any land that is not very conducive to tilling
                        Should be built upon,
    Especially those structures belonging to the community.
The purpose of the community farm
And the semblance of government that peoples and works it,
Is to act as the "supermarket",
    From which be available various packaged—
    Canned or otherwise—foods,
        Generally reserved from past, plentiful harvest(s).
Neither is it necessarily necessary to till the land alone:
Hydroponic growth will suffice for rapid, continuous
production.

For energy, solar power.
    (Of course.)
To till the land, tractors.
                          Why not?
                    Home-made diesel works just fine.
As for meat, animals should generally be allowed to roam free,
    And hunting be a main means of acquiring meat.
As for beef, pork, and chicken,
Private ownership of the living animals would not be
discouraged,
    But generally the community farmers
        Would be in charge of such things,
        Simply because it seems easier that way.
General education is ever free and compulsory;
But higher education I would severely discourage,
    Being instead a proponent of apprenticeships.
…This-all being quite understandable,
    Even nice to consider generally implementing,
What of material goods?
—That is why the commune is but temporary.
Not only does it entail relatively hard labor,
The only thing anyone would have to show for themselves is,
    Well, themselves.
Which is fine and good,
    But what about those who like to read,
    Or play music,
    Or invent new tools,
    Or think,
    Or solve mathematical problems?
Well, let them do it.
    That's what they should do:
    And they teach others, this being their service.

The only way to reject society is to live in a society so far
advanced:
The commune *exists,* as you do,
    For your usage;
    Come to it, but do not take more than it gives,
    And realize it is not necessary to give more than it takes.
In the more general sense,
    The implementation of the ideal is only philosophically
possible.
The world in which we live is the result of:
    The natural progression of things.
Any extreme, in either direction,
    Will only return to the present.
Within the commune, time stops
    Because there is no money,
    There are no real obligations except to Self
    And those to the community
        Are only those imposed by yourself upon yourself,
            By having chosen to be there
            And participate in what fashion you do.
…But we should ever want to return to society,
    Or so it would be presumed;
And if we're going to return to society,
        We'll need some money.
    And if we need that, we'll go to war.
Therefore I live in this capitalist society
                because they died.
        I buy, sell, and trade,
                  in blood.
            So do you…
                So do we all.
For capitalism has that same mandate:

Spread the love;
    Share your message,
        Your ideal;
            We really care,
                                we really do.
            How can you tell?
            'Cause we charge fifty dollars an hour to listen!
Capitalism is the parody of the Roman Catholic Church.
Do as you please,
                    Respecting your fellow man:
I'll help you if you help me,
    Whether in the form of money or service.
Oh. Oh, you're a big
                        *(sinner)*
                            business?
            We'll forgive you.
Oh. Oh! You've saturated the market?
    Well they don't have it
                        *(Christianity)*
                            over *there,* do they?
Oh. The workers are too expensive?
    Well, hire foreigners—Natives to themselves—
    And they work
                    *(confess)*
                        their tails off,
For dirt cheap: You'll make it
                    *(collection)*
                        back in no time!
…The need to be individual,
    To be seen as such,
    And success in being seen,
        Only serves to ensure another's misery.

Actually, one's own:
For, being so individual, single,
One is never part of the group.
Perfect individuality is attained by
Only Mother Nature Herself (if It is a woman),
Where each unit simply makes a part of the whole.
It laughs at us, insofar as Nature is capable:
So many plants and animals in herds, groups:
But is anything really aware of anything much else?
Does any part of the whole care anything much about
another?
And we are working to attain it,
Or perhaps cannot help ourselves,
Since we *are* a part of Its entirety.
Creating to destroy,
                    Destroying to create.
        Flourishing
                    Nourishing
            Wretched
                    And torn:
                        O, Constant Change!


…Marriage,
        Is a somewhat outdated trend.
    If you love each other, why must you so elaborately say
so?
—*Because* you love each other.
    Elsewise, common-law marriage should be generally
recognized.


…The value of life,

In a capitalist society, and knowing what we now think we
know,
    Is always questionable…
        But if you're going to be a capitalist,
            You might as well be pro-choice,
            Since you are just as much a murderer
                As the perceived culprit.

Value of material goods is really quite relative,
    But all that in the by-and-by,
        Subject to the First Knowledge anyway.

…And in the end,
    The only point of doing anything
    Is to consume, transform, and expel,

Energy.
Of the sun
Of God,
Of all that came before,
And of all that is to come.
You are the person ahead of you;
And the one behind.
You are the vehicle in which you ride,

You are the table,
The book,
The tree,
The dog,
The mouse,
The cheese,
The everything.

You are the past,
    You are the present,
        You are the future;
You are your own God;
    You are your own worst nightmare.
You are your own greatest achievement.
        *You are who you are;*
            *I am who I am.*


Then Mageira's energy mingled with itself, and all things,
And his family lived with his words in their heart.


February 2005
February 2008

Tucson, Arizona

# Would you like to see your manuscript become a book?

If you are interested in becoming a PublishAmerica author, please submit your manuscript for possible publication to us at:

**acquisitions@publishamerica.com**

You may also mail in your manuscript to:

**PublishAmerica
PO Box 151
Frederick, MD 21705**

# www.publishamerica.com

CPSIA information can be obtained at www.ICGtesting.com
Printed in the USA
LVOW052007310812

296805LV00001B/56/P